WHERE IS MY COUNTRY?

by Robin Nelson

first step nonfiction

Lerner Publications Company · Minneapolis

I live in a **country.**

A country can have many
cities and **towns**.

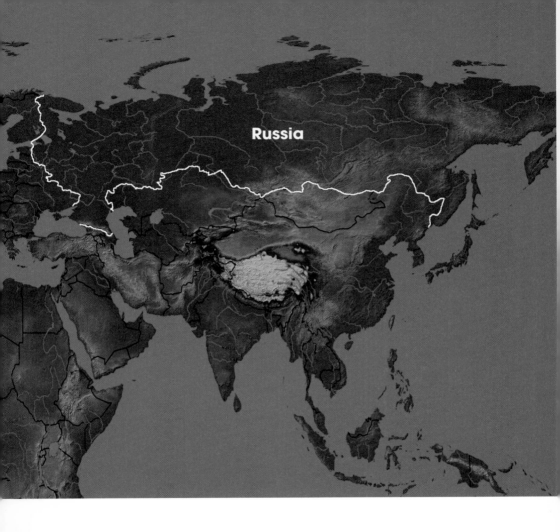

A country can be very big.

The biggest country is bigger
than most **continents**.

Vatican City

A country can be very small.

The smallest country is
smaller than most cities.

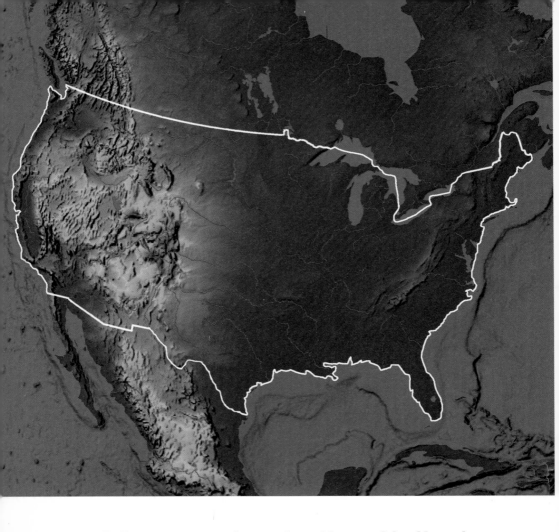

My country is the United
States of America.

Most of my country is on the
continent of North America.

The country of Canada is
north of my country.

The country of Mexico is
south of my country.

There are families living in
countries all over the world.

Some countries have land
on all sides.

Some countries are by the ocean.

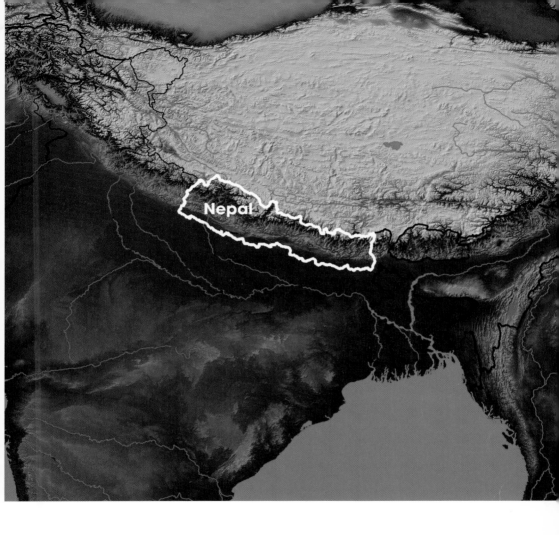

Some countries are by the
mountains.

Where is my country?

My country is on my continent,
where I live with my family.

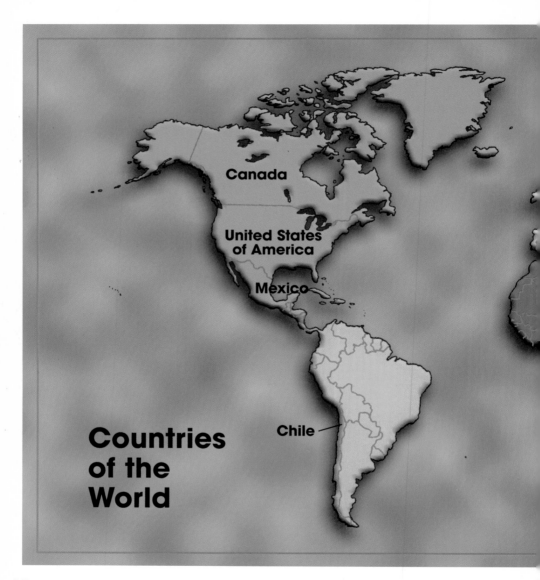

Canada

United States
of America

Mexico

**Countries
of the
World**

Chile

Vatican City

Russia

Nepal

Botswana

19

Country Facts

- The world's smallest country is Vatican City. It is located within another country—Italy.

- The biggest country is Russia. Russia stretches across two continents—Asia and Europe.

- The United States is the third largest country in the world in population after China and India.

- Australia is the only country that is also a continent.

The United States is divided
into 7 regions:
1. New England
2. Middle Atlantic States
3. Southern States
4. Midwestern States
5. Rocky Mountain States
6. Southwestern States
7. Pacific Coast States

 The U.S. bird is the bald eagle.

 The U.S. flower is the rose.

Glossary

cities – places where many people live and work. A city is a large town.

continents – seven large land masses on the earth

country – a place where people live and share the same laws

towns – places where people live and work. A town is smaller than a city.

Index

The photographs in this book are reproduced through the courtesy of: © Earth Imaging/Stone, front cover, p. 9; © Wolfgang Kaehler, pp. 2, 3, 5, 12, 16, 22 (top and bottom); © John Heseltine/Corbis, p. 7; © Earl Kowall/Corbis, p. 10; © M. Bryan Ginsberg, p. 11; © Todd Powell/ Photo Network, p. 17.

Lerner Publications Company
A division of Lerner Publishing Group
241 First Avenue North
Minneapolis, MN 55401 U.S.A.

Website address: www.lernerbooks.com

Library of Congress Cataloging-in-Publication Data

Nelson, Robin, 1971–
    Where is my country? / by Robin Nelson.
      p.   cm. — (First step nonfiction)
    Includes index.
    ISBN: 0–8225–0192–9 (lib. bdg. : alk. paper)
    1. Geography—Juvenile literature. 2. Family—Juvenile literature. [1. Geography.]
I. Title. II. Series.
G133.N37 2002
910—dc21   2001000962

Manufactured in the United States of America
1 2 3 4 5 6 – AM – 07 06 05 04 03 02